How *to* Be *a*
Kingdom
Princess *in a*
Drama Queen World

How *to* Be *a*
Kingdom Princess *in a*
Drama Queen World

Denise Jane Ward

Xulon Press

Xulon Press
555 Winderley Pl, Suite 225
Maitland, FL 32751
407.339.4217
www.xulonpress.com

Paperback ISBN-13: 978-1-66289-719-1
Ebook ISBN-13: 978-1-66289-720-7

Table of Contents

৫১

Introduction

❧

HAVE YOU EVER felt like a princess in a drama queen world? Like you were meant for something more than the petty conflicts, the constant comparisons, and the exhausting pursuit of perfection? As I sit here, I am reminded of the countless women who have journeyed through life feeling trapped by the expectations and demands of the world around them. I, too, have experienced the weight of these pressures, the feeling of constantly trying to fit into a mold that was never meant for me. But in the midst of it all, I discovered a truth that changed everything. *How to be a Kingdom Princess in a Drama Queen World.* It's a title that may sound like a paradox, but one that holds within it the key to unlocking a life of true purpose and freedom. This book is not just another self-help guide or a collection of empty affirmations. It is a journey through the depths of your heart and soul; a rediscovery of your true identity and the power that lies within you.

In today's world, it is easy to get caught up in the busyness, the distractions, and the relentless pursuit of status and success. The pressure to conform to societal norms can be suffocating. We are bombarded with messages that tell us we are not good enough, not pretty enough, and not smart enough while being constantly compared to others. But here is the thing: you were never meant to fit into society's mold. You were created to stand out; to shine brightly in a world that desperately needs your light.

As you journey through the pages of this book, you will discover the truth of who you really are - a beloved daughter of the King; a princess in His kingdom. I invite you to take a moment to close your eyes and imagine a world where drama and chaos fade away; where you are free to be your authentic self without fear of judgment or rejection. Can you see it? Can you feel the weightless freedom of being fully known and fully loved? This book is your passport to that world. It is a roadmap that will guide you through the twists and turns of life, helping you navigate the challenges and obstacles that lie ahead. It is a refuge, a sanctuary where you can find solace and strength amid the storms. Throughout the following pages, I will share with you the wisdom and insights that I have gathered over the years. From the depths of my own experiences and the lessons I have learned along the way, I will offer you practical guidance and heartfelt encouragement. I will dive into the Word of God and uncover the hidden truths that have the power to transform your life.

But let me be clear: this is *not* a book about escaping reality or living in a fairytale. It is about embracing reality, the gritty and messy parts of life, and finding beauty in the midst of it all. It is about living with courage and conviction, knowing that you have a purpose that is greater than any worldly measure of success. This journey will not always be easy. There will be moments of doubt and uncertainty, moments when the weight of the world feels unbearable, but you must hold on and trust in the promises of God for in those moments of surrender and vulnerability, true transformation occurs.

So, are you ready to embark on this journey with me? Are you ready to step out of the drama queen world and embrace your identity as a kingdom princess? If so, then turn the page and let the adventure begin. The road ahead may be unknown, but I promise it is a road that leads to freedom, joy, and a life that is utterly worth living.

Chapter 1

Embracing Your Identity as a Kingdom Princess

*But you are a chosen generation, a royal priesthood, a holy
nation, His own special people, that you may proclaim the
praises of Him who called you out of darkness into His marvelous light;*

1 Peter 2:9 (NKJV)

Discovering Your Royal Heritage

OVER THE YEARS, I have dug deep into my heritage. This was no easy
feat since one side of my family is very hush-hush about the events from
the past, and digging through sites like *Ancestry,* and other related ones,
led to no more information than my immediate family gave me. I came
to determine that there was no royal heritage there or anyone related to
that type of life. I did find some interesting people on the other side of
the family, but again, no royalty.

This was not just about tracking my family tree. I also had to get in
touch with my spiritual side. I dove deep into sacred texts, soaking up

every bit of wisdom and insight. It was in those ancient words that I found the true essence of my royal roots – a connection to something bigger: a divine purpose that gave my existence some serious meaning.

As I kept on exploring, I had an epiphany: being a princess is not just about bloodline or religious beliefs, it is a whole feeling. It is about embodying the qualities of royalty – being real, sticking to your values, and showing some love to others. Being a modern-day princess is not all glitter and tiaras. It means facing the drama queens in your life head-on. It means acknowledging your toxic behavior and taking steps to break free from that nonsense. It means ditching the constant need for approval and embracing your authentic self. It means choosing love over fear, forgiveness over judgment, and being brave enough to stand out from the crowd.

This journey of uncovering my royal heritage changed me. It forced me to confront my fears, heal old wounds, and tap into my true power. I realized that being a princess is not about fancy palaces and looking pretty; it is about being a beacon of light in a world that sometimes feels dark and heavy. It means representing yourself as one of God's princesses. Once I embraced my royal roots, everything shifted. No longer was I caught up in the drama swirling around me. I became this calm force in the storm, spreading good vibes and positivity wherever I went. My purpose became clear: it was all about lifting others up, helping them discover their own royal worth, and making this world a better place to be in.

Let me tell you a secret. This whole royal heritage thing is not the end-game. It is just the beginning. It is a lifelong process of growth, self-discovery, and empowering yourself. It means owning your uniqueness and using it to make a positive impact.

As I reflect on my journey, gratitude fills my heart. I am grateful for the brief wisdom passed down by my ancestors, the teachings that shaped my faith, and the chance to live out my purpose as a princess in a world that sometimes feels like a never-ending soap opera.

I invite you to embark on your own quest to discover your royal heritage. Dig into your family history, dive deep into what moves your soul, and always remember that being a princess is not something given to you;

it is a lifestyle you choose when you choose Christ. Embrace your inner royalty, break free from the drama shackles, and step into your true power. Together, let us make this world a kingdom ruled by love.

Embracing Your Identity in Christ

You know, the whole concept of embracing who we are in Christ is not just something we read about and understand in our heads. It is something that sinks deep into our hearts and becomes a core belief. We are not just ordinary folks aimlessly wandering around in this crazy world. We have been carefully chosen and called by our Creator for something bigger, something greater. To truly grab hold of our identity in Christ, we must dive into His Word like never before. It is in those pages that we discover our true selves and understand the purpose God has for us. That is where we find out just how valuable and significant we are in His eyes. Can you believe it? Just as Psalm 139:14 tells us, "I am fearfully and wonderfully made," we are masterpieces crafted with love and cared by our heavenly Father.

But here is the deal. Reading and studying the Word alone is not going to cut it. We must soak it *all* in. Let those truths marinate in our souls and change the way we think. It is like a feast for our spirits, breathing fresh life into us and bringing our thoughts in line with what Jesus thinks. The more we meditate on God's promises, the more we see ourselves through His eyes rather than through the twisted lens of the world.

Embracing our identity in Christ also means letting go of those old mindsets and behaviors that just do not fit who we really are anymore. The world may try to stick labels on us and shove us into boxes, but we should not have any of it. We should boldly toss those labels aside and fully embrace the unique purpose God has given us. We are not defined by our past mistakes or even our victories; we are defined by the love and grace of our heavenly Father.

Let me tell you something else. Truly embracing our identity in Christ means not seeking validation from others. In a world where everyone is obsessed with getting likes and comments on social media, it can be tempting to crave affirmation. But here is the secret: our worth is not found in the opinions of others; it is rooted in the unshakeable love of our heavenly Father. We can walk confidently in our true selves, knowing that we are fully accepted and cherished by the one who matters most.

As I continue this incredible journey of embracing who I am in Christ, I am reminded of what the apostle Paul said, "I have been crucified with Christ. It is no longer I who live, but Christ who lives in me" (Gal. 2:20 ESV). It is in that surrender, that identification with Christ, that I discover who I really am. I am a beloved daughter of the King, a princess of the kingdom empowered by the Holy Spirit.

My friend, let us continue on this amazing journey of embracing your identity in Christ. Let us dig deeper into His Word, let those truths sink into our souls, and let go of all that old junk we have been carrying around. Together, we can step into the fullness of who God created us to be. We will rise above all of the drama and chaos of this world, shining as radiant princesses of the kingdom, and boldly proclaiming our true identity in Christ.

Overcoming the Comparison Trap

The comparison trap is like a sneaky spider's web. It is this intricate, tangled mess of insecurity, doubt, and fear that is way too easy to get trapped in its sticky grip. Before you know it, it is all you can think about as it starts defining how you see yourself.

As a woman of God who is armed with some knowledge in biblical studies and psychology, I have come to realize that comparisons are not just unnecessary, but downright toxic for our personal growth and overall well-being. When we start comparing ourselves to others, we lose sight of our unique identity. We forget that every one of us is fearfully and wonderfully made by a loving Creator who had us in mind. We were never meant to be cookie-cutter copies of each other, we were made to be masterpieces in our own right, and understanding and embracing this truth is the key to busting out of that comparison trap.

Let us get real for a moment. Overcoming that annoying trap starts with recognizing that our worth and value do not come from what anyone else says or thinks. As a princess in the kingdom, let me tell you that my worth is not determined by the number of likes on some social media post, the size of my waistline, or even the list of achievements on my resume. No, my worth is all about my relationship with God and how I am living out His purpose for my life.

How do we break free from that trap of comparisons? We have to shift our focus from what is happening on the outside to what is going on inside. Instead of obsessing over what others have, we need to channel our energy into becoming the best version of ourselves. Forget about comparing our journey to someone else's. Let us embrace our unique path and give ourselves a round of applause for every bit of progress we make along the way. This change in perspective is what helps us cultivate an attitude of gratitude and contentment, which, in turn, saves us from being suffocated by comparisons.

There is also power in having a good support system. Surrounding ourselves with people who build us up and remind us of our worth is like a secret weapon against falling back into that sticky trap of comparison. When we have a tribe of cheerleaders around us, we are less likely to get tangled up in the web because having people who create a safe space for vulnerability and growth is what helps us fully bloom into the princesses we were meant to be.

As I keep walking this crazy journey as a princess in a world full of drama queens, I am determined to not let this comparison game take over my life. It is not going to happen. Instead, I choose to focus on cultivating a heart of gratitude, celebrating even the tiniest steps of progress, and cherishing the relationships that uplift and inspire me. By doing all of that, I am breaking free from that comparison trap and stepping into my purpose as a kingdom princess. The world out there is begging for every one of us to shine our own unique lights.

Embracing Your Kingdom Authority

As a woman of God, I have always been captivated by the idea of kingdom authority. It is not just some distant concept; it lights a fire deep within my soul. I honestly believe that our authority is a precious gift from God, one that we should never take lightly, so let us dive into the significance of understanding and embracing our authority as kingdom princesses.

To truly grasp the weight of this authority, we first need to understand what it means to be a princess in God's kingdom. We are not just bystanders in this drama queen world; we are daughters of the King of Kings. Our identities are rooted in Him, and our purpose is to bring glory to God and make an impact in the world. We are called to be ambassadors of His kingdom, shining His light and love in even the darkest corners (2 Cor. 5:20).

Embracing our kingdom authority means recognizing the power and influence we possess as children of God. It is an honor and a responsibility. Just like an earthly princess has privileges and responsibilities, so do we in our spiritual kingdom. God has entrusted us with the authority to bind and loose, to decree and declare, and to bring blessings from heaven into the earthly realms (Matt. 18:18).

But with great power comes great responsibility. We cannot just go around wielding our authority to fulfill our own selfish desires. We must submit to His authority and be vessels of His love and righteousness. Our authority is not a weapon to dominate or control; it is a tool to bring healing, restoration, and transformation.

To effectively exercise our authority, we need to surrender ourselves completely to God's authority. We must give Him full control over our thoughts, emotions, and actions, allowing His Spirit to guide and direct us. Our authority flows from our intimate relationship with the King. It is only when we truly abide in Him that we can walk in the fullness of our authority.

Furthermore, embracing our kingdom authority requires a deep understanding of God's Word. We need to immerse ourselves in the truth, allowing it to saturate our hearts and minds. His Word helps us align our thoughts and beliefs with His perspective. It gives us the wisdom and discernment we need to use our authority in a way that brings Him glory and impacts the world for His kingdom.

And lastly, embracing our kingdom's authority demands humility. We must remember that our authority is not something we have earned or achieved on our own; it is a gift given to us by God's grace. We should not exalt ourselves; instead, we should acknowledge that all authority ultimately belongs to Him. As kingdom princesses, our call is to be servant leaders, using our authority to serve and uplift others.

In conclusion, embracing our kingdom's authority is a lifelong journey. It is not a one-time event, but a continuous process of growth and maturity. As we surrender to God's authority, soak ourselves in His Word, and walk in humility, we will begin to see the impact of our authority in the world around us. Miracles will happen, lives will be transformed, and the glory of God will be revealed. We are kingdom princesses, and we have been given the authority to change the world for His glory.

Navigating the Drama of the World

You know how it is, right? Gossip, jealousy, backstabbing, and all of that superficial drama of the world seems to either be thrown at us or lies in wait, ready to pounce on even the best of us. It is like a dark cloud that makes its home in our hearts and minds, messing up our heads and making us lose sight of who we are.

Do not let that drama define you as a princess. All of this drama is just a reflection of people's brokenness and insecurities. It is a cry for attention and validation; a desperate attempt to fill the void inside. And even though the world loves to revel in drama, we must choose to rise above it.

So, the first thing we must do is understand where all of this drama comes from. It is all rooted in brokenness. Knowing that will help us approach it with compassion instead of getting caught up in it. Personally, I am not saying I support or get involved in drama, but that I am all about redemption and healing.

Another key thing in dealing with drama is protecting my heart and mind. It is so easy to get sucked into all that drama and get spun around in its tornado of destruction, but I have learned to be careful with what I let in. I filter my thoughts and keep my speech in check. No gossip or negativity for me. I am all about filling my head with the good stuff, soaking up God's Word, and surrounding myself with uplifting people.

It is all about intentional relationships, too. I have figured out that I have to hang with people who build me up, not tear me down. People who cheer me on and support me, not those who always have something negative to say. These relationships are my lifeboats in the storm; my safe place amid all the craziness. They remind me of who I truly am - a princess in the kingdom - and together, we navigate through the drama with grace and wisdom.

But you know what my secret weapon is? Prayer. When all else fails, I surrender the drama to God. He is the one who can truly heal and restore. I invite Him to work in my heart and in the hearts of others, bringing about change and reconciliation (2 Cor. 5:18). I trust in His guidance and wisdom, knowing He will lead me through those rough patches and into the calm waters of His love.

As a princess in a world full of drama queens, I am choosing to navigate it all with grace, compassion, and strength. I am not going to let the drama define me. I am called to something bigger, to bring light in the darkness, peace in the chaos, and love in the brokenness. By staying grounded in the truth and love of Jesus Christ, I am equipped to handle whatever drama this world throws at me with wisdom and grace.

Time to Reflect

- Write and memorize Psalm 139:14.
- Name three things that make you unique.

- Have you fallen into the comparison trap? If so, name at least one thing that you can do to escape the trap.

Prayer

Dear Lord, I thank You that I am fearfully and wonderfully made. Help me to remember this when the drama seems overwhelming. Please give me strength to be a beacon to others of Your love. Father, I confess that I do not always pay attention to You, but to the world. Help me to become closer to You and to grow in my relationship with You. I pray all of this in Jesus's name. Amen

Chapter 2

Cultivating a Kingdom Mindset

And do not be conformed to this world, but be transformed by the renewing of your mind, that you may prove what is that good and acceptable and perfect will of God.

Romans 12:2 (NKJV)

The Power of Positive Thinking

HAVE YOU EVER stopped to consider the power that lies within your thoughts? It is something that has always fascinated me, and as a woman of faith, I have seen firsthand the incredible impact that positive thinking can have on our lives. It is like a spark that ignites a fire within us, propelling us forward on our journey toward happiness and fulfillment.

Research has shown that our thoughts can directly influence our physical and mental well-being. It is crazy to think that something as simple as a positive mindset can lower our stress levels, improve our heart health, and even boost our immune system.[1] And let us not forget the incredible effect it has on our overall happiness and satisfaction with life.

But how do we cultivate this powerful tool of positive thinking? How do we shift our minds from negativity to optimism, even when faced with challenges?

One of the first steps is to become aware of our thoughts. It is so easy to get caught up in the hustle and bustle of life that we forget to pay attention to the thoughts swirling around in our heads. But by taking a moment to pause and reflect, we can start to recognize patterns of negativity and consciously choose to shift our focus toward more positive and uplifting thoughts.

Another key aspect is surrounding ourselves with positive influences. Just like a flower needs sunlight and nutrient-rich soil to grow, our positive thoughts need nourishment. So, let us seek out those who radiate positivity, immerse ourselves in inspiring books and stories, and listen to motivational speakers who can fill our minds with the fuel to create a positive mindset.

And let us not forget the power of gratitude. It is so easy to overlook the blessings and joys in our lives, especially when we get caught up in the chaos of daily life. But by practicing gratitude and intentionally taking time each day to acknowledge and appreciate the good things, we can train our minds to focus on the positive, even during times of adversity.

I encourage you to embrace the power of positive thinking. Take control of your thoughts and watch as your reality transforms into a kingdom of joy, peace, and fulfillment. It is within your reach, and I believe in you. Together, let us create a life filled with positivity and endless possibilities.

Challenging Negative Beliefs

Beliefs have this crazy way of shaping our lives. They can either lift us up or tie us down. It is wild how something so intangible can have such a hold on us. I have been there, stuck in my own bubble of negative beliefs, feeling trapped in this endless maze of self-doubt and fear. I genuinely believed that I was not good enough, smart enough, or talented enough to achieve my dreams. I let those negative thoughts dictate who I was and what I was capable of. It is like being locked up in a prison you built yourself.

But one day, I realized that only I, with God's help, had the power to break free from this self-imposed mess. It hit me like a lightning bolt that these negative beliefs were more than just holding me back; they were keeping me from becoming the princess I was always meant to be. With that realization, I set out on a quest to challenge those beliefs and transform them for good.

The first thing I had to do was identify those sneaky negative beliefs. I had to bring them out into the open and stare them right in the face. Trust me, it was not easy. They were like these annoying whispers in my ear, telling me I was not good enough or that I would never succeed. But once I started paying attention, I noticed the patterns and triggers that brought them to life. So, I started writing everything down in a journal, keeping a record of my own inner saboteur.

Next came the eye-opening part, digging deep to find out where these beliefs even came from. I had to unravel the origins. Turns out, a lot of them were based on other people's opinions and judgments. I mean, these beliefs were not even mine. They were just projections of the insecurities and fears of the people around me. Honestly, it blew my mind.

Once I had that "aha" moment, I knew I could not let these negative beliefs run the show anymore. It was time to put them to the test, to question their validity. I asked myself, "Is there any real proof to back up these beliefs?" And the answer was a big, fat, "No." They were nothing more than illusions, built on a shaky foundation of misconceptions and distorted self-perceptions. It was time to let go.

Here is the thing about challenging negative beliefs. It is not enough to just shoot them down; you have to replace them with something better, more empowering. So, came the positive beliefs. I filled my mind with affirmations and words that reminded me of my worth, my smarts, and my ability to kick some serious butt. And I made sure to surround myself with a dynamite crew of people who believed in me and pushed me to believe in myself.

Slowly but surely, I rewired my brain. Self-doubt and fear were replaced with confidence and self-belief. I transformed those negative beliefs into determined affirmations that guided my every move. I said goodbye to those limitations that had held me down and said hello to a world of endless possibilities. It was not easy, but it was worth it.

And now, here I stand, a transformed princess in a drama queen world. I do not let those negative beliefs define me anymore. I have tapped into the power within me to create the life I want. And guess what? You can, too. Seriously, no more letting those negative beliefs be in charge. Challenge them, transform them, and step into your kingdom.

Renewing Your Mind with God's Word

As I soaked in every word, a sense of calm flooded over me like a soothing balm for my tired soul. It was like a gentle reminder that I was not alone in my struggles. God's Word became my compass, guiding me through the chaotic ups and downs of life, offering me hope when all seemed hopeless, and giving direction when I felt lost. Renewing my mind was not just some passive thing, though. It required me to actively engage with God's Word. I had to set aside time each day to fully immerse myself in its truths, to dwell on its promises, and to let its wisdom sink deep into my very being. It was only through this intentional pursuit of God's Word that I discovered the key to transforming my mind and renewing my perspective.

Early in the morning, as the sun timidly peeked through my curtains, I would sit in reverent silence, holding my Bible close. Its pages felt weighty as if they were infused with a divine presence. And in those sacred moments, I would breathe in its essence, allowing its truth to penetrate the deepest corners of my soul.

As I began to read, I was awestruck by the richness and depth of the scriptures. It was not just a collection of tales from long ago; it was a living testament to God's character and faithfulness. The stories of those who had gone before me mirrored my own struggles and triumphs, encouraging me and reminding me that God's grace was not limited to some distant past, but extended to the here and now.

Reading was soon not enough. I needed to meditate on these words, to let them take root in my heart. Armed with a pen and a journal, I dove into a journey of contemplation, digging deeper into the words on the page, searching for those hidden pearls of wisdom. I spent time taking in a single verse, holding it to my heart, and memorizing it. As I studied, patterns and themes began to emerge, intertwining through the tapestry of scripture. I saw a relentless God pursuing His people with unending grace. I saw a God who valued justice, mercy, and humility, who called His followers to love and show compassion. Day by day, my mind underwent a total transformation. The doubts and fears that once haunted me faded away, replaced by confidence and assurance that could only come from knowing the Author of life Himself. I clung to the promises of scripture, believing without a doubt that I was fearfully and wonderfully made, chosen, and redeemed by a God who loved me unconditionally.

Renewing my mind with God's Word became my lifeline, a source of strength and stability in a world that often felt like it was falling apart. It was a constant reminder that even in the middle of all of the chaos and drama, I could find peace and rest in the loving arms of my heavenly Father. As I embraced this truth, as I let the truth of God's Word seep into every fiber of my being, I found myself set free from the chains of comparison, insecurity, and self-doubt.

My dear friend, I urge you to carve out time each day to fully immerse yourself in the Word's truth, to meditate on its promises, and to let its wisdom shape every thought you have. I promise you, as you do this, the chaos and drama of the world will pale in comparison to the beauty and truth found within the pages of God's Word. You will become like a princess in a world full of drama queens, walking with confidence and grace.

Guarding Your Thoughts and Influences

Let us now talk about something super important: guarding our precious thoughts and influences. This is a big deal for our thoughts are like the building blocks of our actions and the stuff we let into our lives shapes the way we think. It is crazy how our thoughts can either lift us high up or bring us way down. They have the power to ignite our souls, push us to be our best selves, and own our true identity as kingdom princesses. On the other side, negative and toxic thoughts can totally wreck us, leaving us doubting ourselves and feeling scared and insecure. So, it is crucial to be super mindful of what we let roam around in our minds.

Now, let us talk about influences: the people we hang with, the media we consume, the chit-chats we have, etc. All of it shapes our outlook on life. This world we live in is like a big, bad drama queen, constantly filling our heads with messages that go against what God wants for us. It is a tough gig. That is why we have to be picky about what and who we let into our lives. Are they lifting us up or bringing us down? That is the question we need to ask ourselves.

As we are all most likely familiar with, guarding our thoughts and influences is not a piece of cake. It takes some serious intentionality and discipline. We have to be aware of the voices we listen to, the stuff we watch and read, and even the friends we let get close to us. As kingdom princesses, we have to focus on platforms and conversations that preach truth, righteousness, and values that are good for the soul. It is like spring cleaning for our minds.

It is not just about what we let in, but also about what we push out. We must work on cultivating a mind that is locked into God's stuff. That means praying, meditating on scripture, and even journaling to help us align our thoughts with God's truth. It is like building a fortress in our minds, keeping out all the bad feelings.

And let me tell you, having a crew of like-minded people is a total game-changer. They will be there to pick us up when we are down, keep us in check, and remind us of who we are in God's kingdom. A true support system.

Guarding our thoughts and influences is an ongoing thing. It is not a one-time deal. We have to keep evaluating and discerning what we are allowing in our lives. Because the drama queen world is not backing down. It will throw all sorts of obstacles our way. But with God's help and the support of our people, we can rise above, shining our light in this dark world.

We will be breaking it down even further and talking about the practical steps we can take to guard our thoughts and influences. I am so excited to be on this journey with you, learning how to be a kingdom princess in a world full of drama queens. Let's do this!

Embracing a Kingdom Perspective

Sometimes I wonder what it really means to embrace a kingdom perspective. It is not just some abstract concept or religious jargon; it is about recognizing that I am a woman of God and that my life should mirror His love and grace. It is about realizing that my identity is not tied to all of the drama that is happening around me, but rather to the truth of who God says I am (1 John 3:1).

When I say I am embracing a kingdom perspective, I mean that I am taking the time to align my thoughts, words, and actions with what God says is true. I constantly remind myself that I am fearfully and wonderfully made (Ps. 139:14) and that the Creator of the universe loves me unconditionally. I tune out all the negative voices that try to tear me down and instead, I choose to listen to that voice of truth.

You know, one of the most powerful things about embracing a kingdom perspective is understanding that my worth does not come from what others think of me, but from my Creator (Gen. 1:26). In a world that is always telling us to fit into this or that mold, embracing a kingdom perspective allows me to find my true identity in Christ.

And it is not just about finding my identity; it is also about shifting my focus from the temporary things in life to the eternal. Let's face it, this world is constantly changing and there is always some new drama unfolding. It is so easy to get caught up in all of that, but when I embrace a kingdom perspective, I am reminded that this world is not my home. My purpose is not about seeking success or approval here, but rather about bringing glory to God and advancing His kingdom.

I must be honest, embracing a kingdom perspective is not always easy. It takes a daily commitment to surrender my will to God's, to seek His guidance and wisdom in everything. It means accepting that I am not in control, but God is, and He has a plan for my life that is way beyond anything I can imagine.

I know that in a world full of drama queens, embracing a kingdom perspective may seem like the opposite of what everyone else is doing. But as a woman of God, it is only through embracing this perspective that I find real peace, joy, and fulfillment. It is through embracing a kingdom perspective that I can rise above all of the drama and be the princess that God created me to be.

Time to Reflect

- Take a few minutes to sit back and relax. Think about your mindset. How can you develop a powerful mindset?
- What negative thoughts can you let go of?
- What positive beliefs can you use to offset the negative ones?

Prayer

Father, I come before You today and thank You for all that You have done for me. Please help me to recognize the negative thoughts in my mind and to replace them with positive ones. Give me the strength to avoid the traps of the Enemy. I ask all this in Jesus's name. Amen.

Chapter 3

Walking in Grace and Forgiveness

And whenever you stand praying, if you have anything against anyone, forgive him, that your Father in heaven may also forgive your trespasses.

Mark 11:25 (NKJV)

எ

Extending Grace to Others

HAVE YOU EVER found yourself in a situation where someone has betrayed you, hurt you to the core, or even stabbed you in the back? It is like a punch to the gut. Your first instinct is usually to hit back, get even, or make them pay. But what if I told you there is a better way? What if I told you that by showing them grace, you not only set them free from the weight of their actions, but also set yourself free from the darkness of anger and resentment?

Grace is a crazy concept. It goes against everything we naturally want to do. It means putting aside our pride and our desire for revenge and choosing love and forgiveness instead. It is not easy, but it is crucial for our growth and our soul's well-being. When we show grace to others, we are embodying the love and compassion of Jesus. We are showing the world what He is all about. It is through grace that we reveal the power of the gospel and the boundless love of God.

Realistically, showing grace does not mean letting people off the hook or pretending like nothing happened, it means loving them despite their mistakes and imperfections. It means seeing past their screw-ups and focusing on their worth as sons and daughters of God. Showing grace also requires humility. It means admitting that we are not perfect, that we have messed things up, and that we need forgiveness just as much as anyone else. Once we grasp how much grace God has shown us, it becomes easier to extend that same grace to others.

In my journey of showing grace, I have learned that it is not a one-time thing, but an everyday practice. It is a commitment to love unconditionally, to forgive freely, and to let go of any anger or bitterness. It takes time, prayer, and a willingness to make things right. When we show grace, we open the door for healing and restoration. We create an environment where forgiveness can grow, and relationships can be repaired. It is through grace that we break the cycle of pain and bitterness and make room for a future filled with love and unity.

So, my fellow warriors, I urge you to embrace the beauty of showing grace. Look for opportunities to love those who do not deserve it, to forgive those who need it, and to let go of anything that is holding you back. Remember, as children of the Most High, it is our calling to be messengers of grace in a world that is desperate for it. Let us rise above the drama and walk in the footsteps of our Savior, showing grace to all.

Embracing God's Forgiveness

Do you want to know what forgiveness *really* means? It is not just some fluffy concept; it is a straight-up gift from the big man upstairs. It is like when someone wrongs you, but instead of holding a grudge or seeking revenge, you let it go and restore your soul. It is a crucial part of being human. We all make mistakes; we all stumble and fall. It is just a part of the messy journey we call life. But forgiveness? That is what helps us grow and move forward. It is like an invitation to drop all of the baggage weighing us down and step into a whole new level of freedom.

But you cannot just throw forgiveness around like it is a magical solution. It is not a free pass to keep doing the same dumb stuff and thinking everything is cool. It is more like a wake-up call. It is a mirror that forces us to confront our weaknesses and flaws. It is a chance to take a good hard look at ourselves and make some changes.

When you hit rock bottom, when shame and guilt threaten to swallow you whole, that is when God's forgiveness starts to shine. It is like a big warm hug that gives you the strength to face your past mistakes head-on. And once you have experienced that incredible forgiveness, you cannot help but want to share it with others. It is like a ripple effect, spreading healing and reconciliation wherever it goes.

Don't get me wrong, forgiveness is not always a walk in the park. It takes guts, humility, and a willingness to face your deepest wounds. You have to let go of your pride, surrender control, and trust in a love that is out of this world. In the process, you have to set yourself free from all of that self-condemnation nonsense and let God's love seep into every part of you (Rom. 8:1). You cannot let your past mistakes define you; instead, embrace the never-ending love and grace that is offered to you.

Speaking of my journey, embracing God's forgiveness has transformed my life. It is like this incredible light breaking through the darkest of nights. It has replaced my guilt and shame with a renewed sense of hope and redemption. Now, as I navigate this crazy world, I know deep down that God's forgiveness is not just for me, but for everyone.

So, let us not just keep this beautiful gift to ourselves. Let us be like little love warriors, spreading forgiveness and hope like it is our job. Through our words and actions, let us show the world what grace is all about. We can be the ones to create ripples of forgiveness and reconciliation one act of love at a time (2 Cor. 5:17-20).

We need to open up our hearts and arms and fully embrace God's forgiveness. Let us march forward and leave our past mistakes behind because we have been called to embody the incredible grace and compassion that has been given to us. And may our lives be a testament to the healing power of forgiveness as we journey together toward redemption and transformation.

Forgiving Yourself

Forgiving myself was like trying to scale Mount Everest without any gear. The weight of all of my screw-ups and flaws was like a ton of bricks on my heart, dragging me down into this pit of guilt and shame. It felt like every mistake I made was a permanent stain that I could not scrub away, no matter how hard I tried. And let me tell you, I tried my hardest.

I would get stuck in this vicious cycle of beating myself up, replaying all of my fumbles and flubs over and over in my head. I was my own personal punching bag, constantly hammering myself for not meeting some impossible standard of perfection. It was exhausting. But then, something clicked. I dug deeper into my faith, poured over the Word of God like it was my life's mission, and I had an epiphany: forgiving myself, as crazy as it seemed, was the key to unlocking my true potential as a princess in the kingdom.

I realized that I could not fully embrace my identity as a daughter of the King until I embraced His crazy, mind-blowing grace and forgiveness for myself. It was like this whole weight lifted off my chest. I could breathe again.

The road to self-forgiveness meant facing the root of all of my self-condemnation head-on. It was like sleuthing through the deep dark depths of my soul. I had to finally admit that I had been living off of this distorted view of my worth. I had let other people's opinions and society's messed-up expectations define who I was instead of finding my value in God's unconditional love.

It was a formidable breakthrough. Liberating, yes, but also very scary. I had to rewire my whole sense of identity and ditch these toxic beliefs that had me trapped. It was like breaking free from chains one link at a time.

One thing that helped me in forgiving myself was separating my actions from my worth as a person. I had to grasp that screwing up did not mean I was some colossal failure. Making mistakes just meant I was a human, flawed and all. Guess what? That is okay. God's love for me is not based on my performance; it is based on the fact that I am His masterpiece, created to kick some serious butt.

Another thing that played a huge role in forgiving myself was owning up to my mistakes. I had to take responsibility for my actions and make things right wherever possible. No more avoiding or sweeping stuff under the rug. I had to step up and fix what I messed up. It was not easy, but it was humbling and gave me a fresh start, a clean slate to build upon. I had to show some love to myself, too. I had to treat myself with kindness and compassion, just like I would for my best friend. I had to embrace my strengths and weaknesses, celebrate my wins, and permit myself to grow at my own pace. That was also a hard lesson to learn, but like watering a plant, nurturing it, and watching it bloom, I was blossoming.

Forgiving myself was and continues to be a journey. It is not a one-time thing, but a choice I must make every day. Each morning, I have to release myself from the chains of self-condemnation and soak up the freedom of grace. It is this process that reminds me I am not defined by my past screw-ups. My identity is wrapped up in this epic, boundless love and forgiveness of my heavenly Father. I am on this mission to become a real-life princess in this chaotic world and forgiving myself is part of the plan. It is not a one-time act, but a constant practice of surrendering my flaws to God's unfathomable love and forgiveness. I am discovering who I really am in this wild journey and stepping into this role, this fullness of the princess I was meant to be. It is totally unreal.

Letting Go of Resentment and Bitterness

Listen up, my fellow princesses. I have been through some serious stuff, and let me tell you, resentment and bitterness are no joke. They can mess with your head, suffocate your spirit, and ruin your relationships faster than a bull in a china shop. But here is the thing: we have the power, as women of God, to rise above all of that garbage and find healing and wholeness.

Growing up, I faced my fair share of hardships. Betrayed by so-called friends, rejected left and right - you name it, I have felt it. I held onto that resentment and bitterness like my life depended on it. It ate away at my joy, made me second-guess everyone's intentions, and had me downright jealous of other people's happiness.

Here is what I learned: holding onto all of that negativity only hurts us. Resentment and bitterness are like poison, seeping into our hearts, clouding our judgment, and making everything look dark and gloomy. They trap us in this never-ending cycle of negativity, keeping us from living the incredible life that God has planned for us.

To break free from that toxic grip, I had to confront my pain head-on. I allowed myself to grieve, to feel the weight of my emotions, and then I let it all go. It was not an overnight process, but little by little, I started releasing that baggage.

One of the most important steps for me was forgiving those who had wronged me. Forgiveness was not easy, but I realized that it was necessary for my healing and growth. Holding onto resentment only kept me shackled to the past, preventing me from moving forward. By forgiving those who hurt me, I took back the power they held over my life and invited God in to restore and heal my broken heart (Eph. 4:32).

I realized forgiveness was about forgiving myself, too. We can be our own worst critics, replaying our mistakes and failures in our minds like a broken record. We hold onto guilt and shame like they are our only identity but let me tell you something: God's grace knows no bounds, and His love is unconditional. I had to forgive myself for the mistakes I had made and believe in the life-changing power of God's mercy.

Letting go of resentment and bitterness also required a major shift in perspective. Instead of dwelling on the bad stuff, I started focusing on the blessings in my life, even in the middle of tough times. Every setback became an opportunity for growth and every disappointment became a chance to rely on God's faithfulness. That change in mindset allowed me to see beyond my pain and understand that God was working all things together for my good (Rom. 8:28).

In the process of letting go, I found true freedom. I shed the weight of resentment and bitterness like a heavy coat, and boy, did it feel good. I walked with a lightness of spirit, embracing each day with gratitude and joy. Being a princess in this drama queen world meant living in the freedom that Christ has won for us - breaking free from the chains of negativity and embracing the life of abundance He has laid out for us.

My beautiful sisters, I encourage you to embark on this journey of letting go. Let yourself feel the pain, forgive those who hurt you, and extend forgiveness to yourself. Shift your perspective, start focusing on all the blessings in your life, and above all, lean on God's grace and love as you navigate this transformative path.

Always remember, as princesses in God's kingdom, we are meant to reflect His love and grace. Letting go of resentment and bitterness is not just good for ourselves; it is also a testimony to the incredible power of God's redemption and healing in our lives. So, let it all go and step into the fullness of the abundant life that God has prepared just for you.

Living a Life of Grace and Forgiveness

Growing up, I was never taught about forgiveness and grace as far as God was concerned. When I became a woman of faith, I learned that it was in my DNA to follow the footsteps of Jesus, who was all about showing grace even when I stabbed Him in the back and did Him dirty. There were times when I struggled big time with the whole forgiveness thing thanks to my human nature acting up, but there was this one incident that flipped my understanding of grace and forgiveness upside down. It was a betrayal from someone who was like family to me, someone I put all of my trust in. I cannot even describe the mix of pain and anger that flooded my soul. How was I supposed to find it in my heart to forgive this person who caused me so much hurt?

Amid my suffering, I turned to God for some major soul support. I dove headfirst into prayer and got lost in His Word. That journey taught me more than a thing or two about grace and forgiveness.

Turns out, grace is not some fancy word or a one-time favor, but rather a whole way of living. It is like getting a gift you do not deserve and having the guts to give it right back to others. It is choosing to treat people with kindness, love, and understanding, no matter how messed up they might be. It is about looking beyond their flaws and mistakes and seeing the potential for growth and redemption.

Forgiveness is not just a one-and-done deal either, but rather a constant work in progress that takes guts, strength, and a willingness to let go of all of that bitterness. Here is the deal: forgiving does not mean we let them off the hook or justify their actions; it sets us free from the grip of resentment and lets us find true healing and freedom.

Let me be real with you: living a life filled with grace and forgiveness is harder than trying to squeeze into your high school jeans. It takes considerable effort and a genuine desire to be transformed from the inside out. It means we must drop our pride, ditch the thirst for revenge, and let go of always needing to be right. It is about loving others even when they do not deserve it and trying to make peace whenever possible.

Here is the mind-blowing secret: when we choose this grace and forgiveness route, it is not just about showing love and healing to others; it is about getting a taste of God's crazy-amazing grace. It is like we are unleashing the full force of our identity as princesses of the King, as vessels of God's love in a world that is straight-up starving for it.

So, my dearest reader, I am begging you to jump on this journey of grace and forgiveness. Take a good, long look at all of the struggles and pain you have been through and let God guide you into showering grace on those who have done you dirty. Find your healing by embracing the mind-blowing power of forgiveness and watch as your whole life gets flipped right side up by the redemptive love of our heavenly Father.

Just remember, we were not put on this planet to be mere spectators in a world that is crazy dramatic. We are called to be authentic ambassadors of grace, forgiveness, and love. It is through our actions and choices that we can bring some much-needed healing and restoration to a world that is hungry for God's grace. Step boldly into this journey, my fellow princesses, and let your life scream out to the world the incredible power of grace and forgiveness.

Time to Reflect

- Can you remember a time when someone hurt you? How did you react?
- What were the results of your reaction? If it was negative, how do you think the outcome would have been if you had chosen forgiveness and/or grace?
- Take a few minutes to ask God if you have unforgiveness in your heart. If you do, ask God to help guide you to forgive and/or show grace.

Prayer

Lord, thank You for loving me so much that You want only the best for me. Please help me to search my heart for any unforgiveness or animosity that I have against others. Give me the strength and guidance to let go and forgive those who have hurt me. I appreciate all that You have done and continue to do in my life. I pray this in Jesus's name. Amen.

Chapter 4

Finding Strength in the Midst of Trials

I can do all things through Christ who strengthens me.

Philippians 4:13 (NKJV)

The Power of Perseverance

IT IS LIKE survival of the fittest in this world full of drama queens. You have to have that never-give-up attitude, that perseverance to make it through the madness, like being an anchor in a storm or a small guiding light when everything seems pitch-black.

Perseverance is not just something with which you are born; it is a skill you must develop and nurture over time. It is like building up your strength and toughness with each obstacle you face. It is the art of never backing down, no matter how tough things get. It is also about finding purpose in the face of adversity, finding that reason to keep going even when you are knee-deep in doubt and despair. It is about knowing that every setback is just another step toward growing into the person you are meant to be.

But how on earth do you tap into that power of perseverance? It all starts with having the right mindset; genuinely believing that no challenge is too big to conquer (Phil. 4:13) and understanding that failure is not a sign of being a screw-up, but rather a chance to learn and grow. With that kind of mindset, you can take on any hurdle with unshakable determination, knowing that success is not a matter of if, but when.

When life throws obstacles in your path, it is so easy to get caught up in the mess and lose sight of what really matters. That is when we must take a step back, gather our thoughts, and remember why we are actually here. What drives us? What is our ultimate goal? By reflecting on those questions, we find the strength to push through, rise above the chaos, and stay true to ourselves.

Perseverance is not a journey you have to travel alone. Surround yourself with folks who lift you up and inspire you. When you have a community of like-minded people behind you, it is like you have a superhero squad ready to conquer anything. Through shared experiences and wisdom, we find comfort in knowing we are not alone. Together, we can lift each other up, building our strength and commitment to keep on pushing forward.

As I sit here and pour my heart out, I cannot help but think of all the crazy challenges I have faced on my journey. Every single one tested me to my limits, pushing me to face my deepest fears. But do you know what? Through it all, I have discovered this inner strength I never knew I had. It is that strength that came from never giving up and persevering through it all. It has transformed me from just being a bystander in this drama-filled world into someone who takes control of her own destiny.

In a world that loves drama queens and chaos, I have learned to rise above it all and reclaim my identity as a princess in my own right. With the power of perseverance, I have tapped into this well of strength that allows me to soar above the drama and fully embrace my true purpose. As I continue this wild journey, armed with all of the lessons and understanding I have gained, I know deep down that I will not just survive, I will thrive. I will be that beacon of grace, resilience, and unshakable perseverance.

Trusting God in the Storm

Understanding what it means to trust God in the storm is like peeling back the layers of an onion. There is so much more to it than we realize. Trust is this fragile thread that weaves through our very souls, connecting us to something bigger than ourselves. It is not just putting our confidence in some temporary fix; it is about placing our trust in the Creator of the universe, who is solid and everlasting.

Picture the storm. It is like a massive whirlwind of trouble and hardship that is ready to tear us to shreds. It could show up as sickness, money problems, broken relationships, or the crushing weight of shattered dreams. These are the moments when our faith is really put to the test. We are faced with a choice: do we let fear and doubt overpower us, or do we anchor ourselves in the hope of God's promises?

Trusting God in the storm means relying on His character and knowing deep down that He is faithful. It is like an active surrender, a choice to let go and let God take control. I have learned that trust is a continual process of letting God guide us through the chaos, not just a one-time thing. Even in the midst of the storm, God is right there with us, like a lighthouse in the middle of crashing waves. His Word becomes our anchor, keeping us grounded when everything feels like it is falling apart. He never wavers, no matter how dark things get. He is always there, promising to lead us through the storm and bring us to a place of peace.

Trusting God also means surrendering our own expectations and understanding. His ways are beyond our comprehension. Sometimes, we question His timing or doubt His goodness, but it is in those moments that our trust grows stronger. We learn to hold on to His promises, even when they seem out of reach because we know deep down that His plans for us are always for our own good.

So, how do we trust God in the storm? It is all about fostering a deep-rooted faith. It means praying, worshiping, and building a personal relationship with Him. It is leaning into His embrace, finding comfort in His presence, and giving Him our fears and worries. When we trust Him, we can endure any storm that comes our way because we know the one who formed the mountains and crafted the oceans is right there by our side, ready to calm the storms and bring us to safety (Ps. 65:7).

Trusting God in the storm is a bit of a paradox. It is a surrender, but also an empowerment. It is realizing that in our weakness, we find strength, and by relying on Him, we uncover the fullness of life He has for us. So, let us step courageously into the storms ahead, knowing that we walk hand-in-hand with the one who can quiet the fiercest tempests and lead us to the other side. In Him, we find our refuge, our peace, and our unshakable hope.

Overcoming Fear and Anxiety

Fear and anxiety have always been two tricky emotions for me. They sneak up on me like unexpected guests, leaving me with a knot in my stomach and a racing heart. Fear is that gut-wrenching feeling that grips you, making it hard to breathe. It is like a dark cloud hanging over your head, foretelling doom and disaster. And anxiety is that constant nagging worry whispering in my ear, never letting me fully enjoy the present moment.

I have come to realize that fear and anxiety often stem from the unknown. We are scared of what we cannot control or understand, and our minds love to paint vivid pictures of worst-case scenarios. It is like living in a never-ending loop of worry and apprehension. But do you know what? I have discovered a way to break free from these shackles. As a princess of the kingdom, I have the power to overcome these fears by embracing the truth of God's Word.

Isaiah 41:10 (NKJV) is one verse that has helped me through it all and speaks to me on a deep level, "Fear not, for I am with you; be not dismayed, for I am your God. I will strengthen you, yes, I will help you, I will uphold you with my righteous right hand." This verse reassures me that I am not alone in my struggles. God promises to be by my side, giving me strength and support when fear and anxiety come knocking.

Just knowing this truth is not enough, though. We need to put our faith into action. I started by challenging those irrational thoughts that fueled my fears. I asked myself, "Hey, what evidence do I have to support these fears?" I found that there was no logical reason to be afraid. It was all just a mental game I was playing with myself.

Next, I turned to prayer. I poured out my fears and anxieties to God without holding anything back. I asked for wisdom and guidance, begging Him to help me let go of control and trust in His plan for my life. Through prayer, I stumbled upon a peace that defies explanation. It was that calm in the storm, knowing that God is in charge, steering the ship.

Let us not forget about gratefulness, a powerful weapon in the fight against fear and anxiety. By shifting my focus to the blessings in my life and expressing gratefulness for them, I was able to change my perspective. Suddenly, the world did not seem so scary anymore. I started seeing God's faithfulness and provision in every little thing around me.

Overcoming fear and anxiety is an ongoing process. It takes consistent effort and a whole lot of faith. But as a princess of the kingdom, I am confident in the power of God's love and grace to transform my life. Fear and anxiety no longer have a hold on me. I choose to live a life of courage and faith, fully aware that I am a cherished child of God, destined for greatness in His kingdom.

Finding Purpose in Pain

Looking back at my life, it is crazy to think about all of the trials and tribulations I have been through. Growing up in a dysfunctional home was no joke. I had a front-row seat to my parents' struggles and sufferings with all of the emotional turmoil that came with it. I was just a kid, but I ended up becoming the caregiver, trying to hold my family together while feeling the weight of their pain on my shoulders.

Amid all of that chaos, I could not help but wonder why I had to go through all of that suffering. What was the point? How could anything good come out of such heartache? These questions ate away at me, and I found myself desperately searching for answers deep within myself.

As I dug into scripture and dove into my faith, something clicked. I started to see that pain can actually change you for the better. It breaks down all of the walls you build up and shows you just how vulnerable and human you are. It forces you to face your demons head-on and confront all of the darkness lurking in your own heart. That self-examination was not easy. I had to let myself feel every ounce of pain and emotion, not push it away or pretend it did not exist. I had to embrace it all as part of my journey. Truth be told, it is only when we face our pain head-on that we can start to heal and grow.

Pain has this way of stripping away all of the surface-level stuff in our lives. It gets right down to the core of who we really are. It reveals our deepest desires and longings, the ones we usually hide away in our pursuit of success and happiness. When you are in the middle of that anguish, you cannot help but confront your true purpose and the path you are meant to walk.

Through all of my pain, I came to realize that life is not just a series of random events, but more like a beautiful tapestry, intricately woven by a loving and sovereign God. Every challenge and trial we face has a bigger purpose, leading us closer to our true identity and calling. Pain, when approached with faith, becomes a steppingstone to fulfillment and purpose, even destiny itself.

In the midst of my own pain, I somehow found the strength to forgive those who hurt me and let go of all of the weight threatening to swallow me whole. I learned that true freedom is not found in denying or avoiding pain, but in embracing and allowing it to shape us into better versions of ourselves.

Nowadays, as I stand here as a princess in a world full of drama queens, I refuse to let my pain define me. Instead, I see it as the fuel that ignites my purpose in life. Going through all of that suffering has given me this deep empathy for others who are hurting. It has allowed me to reach out with love and compassion to those who need it most.

Finding purpose in pain is not easy. It takes guts to face your deepest wounds and commit to growth even when life throws you curveballs. But as I continue on this crazy journey, I am filled with hope and a renewed sense of purpose because I know that, even in the darkest seasons of life, there is a divine purpose waiting to be uncovered. And that purpose holds the key to unlocking our true identity and calling as princesses in a world full of drama queens.

Thriving in the Midst of Trials

Trying to navigate through tough times can be a real pain in the butt. It is like getting caught in a whirlwind of negative emotions - frustration, anger, despair – that have all come out to play. But being a woman of God, I have learned to see these trials as excellent opportunities for growth and refinement. It is like being that lump of coal that gets squashed under pressure, and then bam! You come out as a diamond, resilient and shining bright.

It can be a challenge to maintain your cool when everything around you is falling apart. It is so tempting to let your emotions take over and spiral into drama and self-pity. Fortunately, I stumbled upon this gem of a verse that says, "From the ends of the earth, I cry to you for help when my heart is overwhelmed. Lead me to the towering rock of safety, for you are my safe refuge, a fortress where my enemies cannot reach me." (Ps. 61:2-3 NLT). By grounding myself in the truth of God's Word, I can find peace amid the chaos and stay strong when facing those trials head-on.

Just like a princess takes care of her mind, body, and soul, I have come to realize the importance of putting myself first during these trying times. That means reaching out to my trusted friends and mentors for support, doing things that bring me joy and a sense of calm, and most importantly, nurturing my relationship with God through prayer and meditation. When I take the time to take care of myself, I am better prepared to handle whatever comes my way.

What has made an enormous difference for me is gratitude. It is so easy to get sucked into focusing on the bad parts of trials and forgetting about all of the wonderful blessings that are still around. But when I intentionally choose to have a grateful heart, everything seems to change. I shift my perspective and find joy even in the middle of the storm. When I start counting my blessings - the lessons learned, the strength gained, and the growth experienced - I realize that trials are here to make me stronger and more compassionate, not to break me down.

Looking back on my journey, I am thankful for the trials I have faced. They have molded me into the woman I am today - a strong, resilient daughter of the King. So, my fellow princesses, I want to encourage you to embrace your trials with bravery and resilience. See them as chances to grow, navigate them with grace and humility, prioritize self-care, and most importantly, cultivate a grateful heart. Trust me, by doing all of that, you will not just survive the trials, you will thrive in the midst of them and become a beacon of hope and strength in a world that is always drowning in drama.

Time to Reflect

- What can you do to develop perseverance?
- What fears and anxieties do you face?
- How can you challenge these fears and anxieties?

Prayer

Father, thank You for sending Your Son here to Earth to die for my sins. Help me to develop perseverance so that I may live my life to the best of my ability. Please help me to take the time to listen to You and learn what is from You and what is from the Enemy. I want to live my life without fears and anxieties. Help me to challenge and replace them with thoughts from Your Word. I pray this in Jesus's name. Amen.

Chapter 5

Building Healthy Relationships

*Make no friendship with an angry man, and with a furious
man do not go, lest you learn his ways and set a snare for
your soul.*

Proverbs 22:24-25 (NKJV)

Understanding Healthy Relationships

TO REALLY GRASP what it means to have a healthy relationship, we
have to break it down, strip away all of the fancy words, and get to the core
of what it is all about. So, a healthy relationship is built on respect, trust,
and open communication. It is like this bond that feeds our emotions
and helps us grow as individuals. In a healthy relationship, you feel safe
to let out your thoughts, feelings, and even your vulnerabilities without
worrying about being judged or rejected. It is like this partnership that
makes you feel connected and supported while still letting you shine as
your own person.

But let us not sugarcoat the fact that healthy relationships are not
exempt from problems. You are going to face all kinds of challenges being

a princess in a crazy, complicated world, right? Well, the same goes for our relationships. The difference with healthy ones, though, is that you and your partner can weather the storm together and come out even stronger. It is all about finding common ground and resolving conflicts with understanding and compassion.

Now, it is not just about having a textbook definition of a healthy relationship. We have to consider that we are all unique individuals with our own experiences and opinions. What might work for one person might not do it for another. It is all subjective.

Speaking of which, I have come to realize that being the princess of my own kingdom means I have to focus on my own personal growth and self-awareness if I want to have healthy relationships. I need to understand what I want and what I stand for so I can come into any relationship feeling secure in myself. It is all about making conscious choices that align with my growth and well-being.

And a healthy relationship does not just magically happen. It takes work, just like taking care of a kingdom. You have to invest time and effort into making that deeper connection, exploring your shared interests, and supporting each other's dreams. It is like the secret sauce to keeping a relationship healthy and thriving.

In the end, understanding healthy relationships is an ongoing journey. It is about getting to know yourself better, being empathetic, and intentionally nurturing that connection. It is all about being able to handle the drama of life together like a boss. So, let us all strive to be these formidable kingdom princesses in this wild, unpredictable world and build relationships that bring us joy, love, and fulfillment.

Effective Communication

When it comes to communication, there is this one thing that sets the tone for how things go down: active listening. Most of the time, we are too caught up in our own heads, ready to jump in with our own opinions without really getting where the other person is coming from. But as a princess, it is my responsibility to prioritize understanding and empathy. I have got to give my full attention not just to the words being said, but to the emotions and desires that might not be said out loud. I want to create a safe space for people to open up where they do not have to worry about being judged or interrupted.

Then there is the power of our words. Being a woman of God, I know how much our words can impact others. I try my best to speak with grace and kindness, steering clear of harsh or critical language that might put people on the defensive or hurt their feelings. My goal is to build people up and bring understanding and resolution instead of stirring up drama.

But it is not just about what we say, how we say it is just as important. As a princess, I have learned the importance of body language, facial expressions, and tone of voice. It is all about making sure everything lines up with what we are saying, so people can really trust our intentions. I keep eye contact to show I am really paying attention and that I trust them. I try to keep a calm and gentle tone, even when things get crazy. It is all about creating a sense of peace and harmony, even in the middle of chaos. Trust me, it makes a difference.

Now, let us talk about trust. It is like the foundation of any relationship, and it only comes with open and honest communication. As a princess, I am all about being real and vulnerable. I am not afraid to share my thoughts and feelings no matter how others might react. This, in turn, encourages others to do the same. It creates an environment where people can be themselves and feel safe. That is what builds trust, and trust is what keeps us all together, even when drama is trying to tear us apart.

Lastly, we have to talk about conflicts. They are going to happen no matter what, but as a princess, I tackle conflicts with grace and my goal is to find common ground. I listen to everyone involved without any biases and I make sure everyone has a chance to say their piece, but then I have to bring everyone back together and find a compromise that works for everyone. It is not always easy, but approaching conflicts with humility and understanding can help us grow and become closer.

When it comes to this whole drama queen world we live in, I hold tight to the principles of effective communication. Listening, choosing my words wisely, showing sincerity through my nonverbal cues, building trust with transparency, and resolving conflicts with grace are my secret weapons to rise above all of the drama. With these tools, I can bring harmony, understanding, and lasting relationships to the table.

Setting Boundaries

Back in the day, boundaries were like some foreign concept to me. I was all about making everyone happy, putting their needs ahead of mine, and sacrificing my own happiness in the process. That kind of behavior, however, is not sustainable. It took me going on this crazy journey of self-discovery and spiritual growth to realize that setting boundaries was not only essential for self-care, but also for honoring God's plan for my life.

Setting boundaries starts with being self-aware and digging deep within yourself. You have to figure out what you need, what you want, and where your limits are, then you have to speak up and communicate those things to the people around you. Sure, it might feel a little uncomfortable or even selfish at first, but it is crucial for your emotional, mental, and spiritual well-being. You cannot pour from an empty cup. By setting boundaries, you are replenishing your own reserves so you can keep serving God and others with all of your heart.

One major part of setting boundaries is knowing when to drop that little word "no." Believe me when I say that saying "no" can feel like you just unlocked a whole new level of empowerment. It lets you assert your needs and limitations without feeling an ounce of guilt or shame. Saying "no" does not mean you are being rude or unkind. It just means you are valuing yourself and recognizing that you have limits. It is all about prioritizing what truly matters and preventing yourself from burning out.

But wait, there is more. Setting boundaries also means communicating them effectively. You have to have those open and honest conversations where you express your needs, limits, and expectations like a boss. Remember this: boundaries are not about trying to control or manipulate others; they are about protecting and taking care of yourself. So, when you communicate your boundaries with love and respect, you are inviting others to do the same. That is how you build healthy relationships.

There will be times when people resist or test your boundaries, pushing the limits you have set, but when that happens, you have to stay firm and confident. Trust me, you are honoring yourself and your journey as a fearsome kingdom princess when you set and enforce those boundaries. It is not about changing or fixing others; it is about taking responsibility for your own well-being.

Here is the bottom line: setting boundaries is necessary in this crazy drama queen world we live in. It is all about showing yourself some love and respect while also building healthy relationships with those around you. As a kingdom princess, you have to establish and enforce boundaries that line up with God's plan for your life. That is how you create a space where you can thrive and fulfill that divine purpose of yours.

Recognizing and Addressing Toxic Relationships

I have come to realize that toxic relationships are just like poison. They come at us all cute and loving, but they slowly drain us of our energy, mess with our self-worth, and make us feel trapped and manipulated. It is like they thrive on controlling us, being jealous, and playing mind games, leaving us no room to grow and be happy.

I have been studying human behavior and spirituality for a while now and understand toxic relationships can take on all kinds of shapes and forms. It could be a partner who emotionally abuses us, always making us feel like we are worthless and under their control. Or it could be a so-called friend who cannot help but bring us down every time we achieve something great, leaving us doubting our own abilities.

No matter how you slice it, toxic relationships are like a blow to our emotional well-being. They tear away our confidence, mess with our perception of reality, and leave us feeling empty and drained. But here is the kicker: the first step in dealing with these toxic relationships is to recognize them.

Yes, recognition starts with us looking at ourselves in the mirror and admitting what is going on. Are we constantly walking on eggshells, scared to set off their anger? Do we always put our needs on the back burner just to keep the peace? Are we left feeling like a pathetic wreck after every interaction with this person? If the answer is yes to any of these questions, then guess what? We are in a toxic relationship.

Recognizing it is just the beginning. We have to summon up the guts to confront it head-on. That means setting boundaries and standing up for what we need and want. It could mean reaching out for professional help or counseling to navigate the messiness of the relationship. It might even involve cutting that person completely out of our lives for the sake of our own sanity.

Now, dealing with a toxic relationship is not easy. It takes real strength, resilience, and a whole lot of belief in our own worth. But we have all got the power to break free from these messed-up patterns and create healthy, fulfilling relationships.

As princesses in this drama queen world, we must spot those toxic relationships no matter how deeply they are woven into our lives. We deserve to be surrounded by people who uplift us, respect us, and push us to be our best selves. Let us take back our power and make our emotional health a priority by dealing with and healing from these toxic relationships. In doing so, we can step into our destiny and be the remarkable women of God that we were always meant to be.

Cultivating Meaningful Connections

Let me tell you a little something about cultivating meaningful connections. It is not always easy, especially in a world where drama queens are clamoring for attention and validation at every turn. But let me also tell you that it is worth it. There is a significant difference between those superficial, self-serving connections and the real deal (the kind that fills your soul and leaves you feeling fulfilled).

To cultivate those meaningful connections, you have to put in the time and effort. I am not just talking about a surface-level understanding here. You have to dig deep. You have to truly listen and be genuinely curious about others' experiences and perspectives. It is not enough to just blab on about your own thoughts and stories. You have to open up your heart and mind to learn from and connect with the people you meet on this crazy journey of life.

Setting healthy boundaries is another key ingredient in this whole connection-making process. Rather than get caught up in the demands and expectations of others, especially in a drama queen world, we, as kingdom princesses, have to prioritize our well-being. We have to make sure we have enough time and energy to nurture and care for ourselves while also forging those real, meaningful connections.

My friend, vulnerability is scary, but it is necessary for those genuine connections. I get it, the world loves masks and facades, but that is not how we are going to find the real deal. We have to muster up the courage to be seen and known for who we truly are. It is through our flaws, struggles, and imperfections that we create those deep and authentic bonds with others.

And let us not forget about forgiveness and grace. In this drama queen world, conflicts and misunderstandings are bound to happen, but instead of holding grudges and seeking revenge, let us be the bigger person. Choose forgiveness and grace. It is not just about freeing the other person from guilt, but about freeing ourselves from the chains of anger and resentment. Trust me, it is liberating.

As I continue on this journey as a kingdom princess in a drama queen world, I am reminded that deep down, we all crave those connections. We all long for something real, something that goes beyond the superficial, and it is up to us to make it happen. By differentiating between the authentic and the shallow, investing in understanding and empathy, setting healthy boundaries, embracing vulnerability, and practicing forgiveness and grace, we can create a world where authenticity and connection flourish. Let us celebrate being kingdom princesses, my friend, and not let the drama overshadow our light.

Time to Reflect

- What are some key points that make up a healthy relationship?
- Why is trust such an important part of any relationship?
- What are three things that you need and/or want from a relationship?

Prayer

Dear Father, thank You for all that You do for me. Help me to learn to stand up for myself regarding boundaries and relationships. Give me Your strength to understand what constitutes a good relationship versus a bad one. Thank you for caring so much about me that You want me to have the best in my relationships. Help me to hear Your voice and accept what You want for me.

I pray this in Jesus's name. Amen.

Chapter 6

Embracing Inner Beauty and Self-Care

But the Lord said to Samuel, "Do not look at his appearance or at the height of his stature, because I have rejected him; for God does not see as man sees, since man looks at the outward appearance, but the Lord looks at the heart."

1 Samuel 16:7 (NASB)

Rediscovering True Beauty

LET US KICK off this journey by ripping apart all of the lies society has shoved down our throats. We have been brainwashed to believe that beauty is all about how we look on the outside (the size of our waist, the shape of our face, how silky smooth our skin is, etc.), but let me tell you that true beauty goes way deeper than that surface-level junk.

Real beauty is like this inner glow that comes from a heart filled to the brim with love, kindness, and compassion. It is about how we treat others, the words we choose to let roll off of our tongues, and the actions we take to lift people up. It is about having the confidence to stand tall, knowing that we were made with nothing short of divine happiness and greatness.

Rediscovering true beauty requires us to shift our focus from the outside to the inside. It means realizing that our worth is not determined by some dumb number on a scale or the amount of makeup we plaster on our faces; it is about our character, values, and how we bring some light to this dark world.

To get this journey started, we have to connect with our inner selves. Picture this: find a cozy little spot, close your eyes, and just let all of the noise of the world fade away. Get lost in your own mind, in a place of peace and calm. Let yourself feel the warm embrace of God's love and acceptance.

While we are connecting with ourselves, it is crucial to embrace self-love and self-acceptance. Love every single part of yourself – from the incredible qualities that make you you to the ugly scars from the bad you have delivered or received - because it is those imperfections that make you shine the brightest, my friend.

To truly rediscover true beauty, we have to soak up positive vibes like a sponge. Surround yourself with people who see your beauty beyond all of the surface stuff, who lift you up and make you feel like a rockstar. Do things that make your soul sing: get lost in a book, throw paint on a canvas, just chill in nature. Surround yourself with beauty, too. Let it remind you how amazing you really are.

Here is the catch: true beauty is not some final destination you stumble upon; it is more like a journey that lasts a lifetime. There are going to be days when you feel awful, when you question your worth and compare yourself to others. In those moments, remember the truth – that you were made with love and grace, and your beauty is a reflection of that.

As we dive into this rediscovery of true beauty, we will soon realize that it is not just one single definition. It is like this wild kaleidoscope of colors, shapes, and forms. It is about embracing diversity and celebrating our one-of-a-kind selves. It is about having the power to light up the world. So, go ahead and embrace that real beauty because it is a gift that is meant to be shared with the whole planet.

Nurturing Self-Worth

Nurturing self-worth requires us to dig deep and get in touch with ourselves. We have to understand that our worth is not dictated by what others think or say about us. We are all fearfully and wonderfully made by a Creator who put so much thought into crafting us. He made us in His own image (Gen. 1:27). That means we are inherently valuable, no matter what anyone else thinks.

Cultivating a healthy inner dialogue is a whole other beast. We are so quick to tear ourselves down, always focusing on what we are not good at and what we lack, but as a woman of God, I am learning that I have to change that narrative. I must bring in some positivity and remind myself of the truth. I am God's masterpiece, created for greatness. He did not hold back when He gave me unique gifts and talents. So, I am flipping the script and focusing on my strengths instead of my weaknesses. I am showering myself with words of love and affirmation because that is what I deserve.

And just to bring up what I have mentioned already, surrounding ourselves with uplifting people is a paradigm shifter. In a world where it feels like everyone's trying to bring you down, finding those mentors, friends, and communities who cheer you on is everything. I have found my tribe of kingdom princesses who remind me of how much I am worth. Those ladies celebrate my wins and hold my hand through the tough times. They helped me navigate this crazy world with grace and resilience, and I could not be more grateful.

Taking care of ourselves is another biggie. We have to give a little love to our bodies, minds, and souls. For me, it is all about doing what brings me joy and feeds my spirit. Whether that is hiking in nature, pouring my heart out in a journal, giving myself some spa-like self-care, or just catching up on some much-needed rest. It is not selfish; it is necessary. I deserve this TLC (tender loving care) because I am a cherished daughter of the King.

But when we truly know our worth, we can see it in others, too. It is like a ripple effect. As a kingdom princess, I strive to show kindness, compassion, and respect to everyone I meet because they are valuable, too. They deserve love and grace just like we do. And when we build others up and help them realize how worthy they are, it just solidifies our worth even more. It is a beautiful cycle, and I am all for it.

In this wild and crazy world, nurturing self-worth is a constant battle, but a battle worth fighting. As a woman of God, I am committed to constantly reminding myself of my inherent worth, shaping my mindset into a positive one, surrounding myself with uplifting people, taking care of me from head to toe, and showing love and grace to others. It is not just about me; it is about inspiring others to find their worth and embrace it, too. We can crush this drama queen world together and stand tall as kingdom princesses because we are beloved daughters of the King.

The Power of Self-Care

Ah, the power of self-care is a concept that often gets forgotten in the chaos and drama of our world, but it is so important. Let me break it down for you. Self-care is all about taking care of ourselves physically, mentally, and emotionally. It is about making ourselves a priority because we cannot give our all when our cup is empty.

And in the middle of a busy princess's life, self-care becomes even more crucial. We are out there trying to serve everyone else and meet all of these expectations, but we forget that we need to take care of ourselves, too. We get so wrapped up in our roles and what is expected of us that we forget about our own needs. Let me assure you that self-care is a *necessity*, not a luxury. It is the key that unlocks our personal growth and empowerment.

Let us dive deep into the power of self-care. It is not just about treating yourself to spa days and shopping sprees (although those can be nice); self-care goes way beyond that. It is about digging deep and getting to know ourselves on a whole new level. It is about facing our fears and limitations head-on and making choices that honor who we truly are.

First, we must take care of our physical well-being. As princesses, we are expected to be strong and graceful, but how can we do that if we neglect our bodies? Our bodies are our temples, and it is our duty to honor and care for them (1 Cor. 6:19-20). Self-care starts with listening to our bodies and giving them what they need (eating when we are hungry, getting enough sleep, and staying hydrated). It means nourishing ourselves with healthy food and getting some exercise. Most importantly, it means allowing ourselves to rest and recharge when we need it without feeling guilty about it.

Next, we must take care of our minds and emotions. As princesses, our minds are powerful tools, but sometimes, our responsibilities, and the negativity around us, can cloud our thoughts. To truly take care of ourselves in this realm, we need to practice mindfulness and find inner peace. This can mean meditating on scripture, journaling, or doing things that bring us joy and relaxation. It also means setting boundaries in our relationships, surrounding ourselves with positive people, and seeking help when we need it. Self-care in our mental and emotional well-being also means being kind to ourselves. It means catching ourselves when we are being too hard on ourselves and replacing those negative thoughts with positive ones. It means acknowledging our emotions and allowing us to feel them without judgment.

At the end of the day, self-care is an act of love toward ourselves. It is a way to show that we deserve kindness and nurturing. It is a commitment to our own growth and well-being. And the beautiful thing is, when we take care of ourselves, we are better able to take care of others, too. So, my dear princess, embrace the power of self-care and let it be the foundation on which we build our kingdom. Only then can we truly shine our light on the world.

Embracing Rest and Balance

Rest is a conscious decision we make to recharge and rejuvenate ourselves. Rather than just taking a break from work or an activity, we have to give ourselves permission to step away from the craziness of life and take the time to replenish our body, mind, and soul. Like self-care, rest is a *necessity* for our well-being, not a luxury.

And then there is balance. It is all about finding harmony in every aspect of our lives. Figuring out when to say yes and when to say no, setting boundaries that are good for us, and putting the things that really matter at the top of our priority list. It means taking a good hard look at what is important to us and making choices that align with our values and goals. Finding that perfect sweet spot where we can chase our dreams, meet our responsibilities, and still have some time for ourselves.

We live in a world that constantly demands our attention and pulls us in a million different directions. It can be hard to slow down and take care of ourselves, but it is possible. We just have to remember that we are human beings, not human doings. Our worth is not defined by how much we accomplish or how busy we are. We have to give ourselves permission to put on the brakes, take a breather, and focus on what really matters.

Another thing we need to let go of is the fear of missing out or falling behind. We have to trust that the world will not come crashing down if we take a step back and put our well-being first. We need to stop constantly feeling like we have to prove ourselves and start focusing on what truly brings us joy and fulfillment.

In this world that is all about drama and being the center of attention, we can change the script. We have the power to live intentionally, to embrace rest and balance as vital parts of our lives. It is not about being lazy or slacking off; it is about finding a healthy rhythm that allows us to thrive. Believe it or not, by actually taking the time to recharge, we will be even more effective and productive in the long run.

So, let us reclaim rest and balance as the princesses we are. Set an example for those around us, showing them that it is possible to live a fulfilling life without sacrificing our well-being. Prioritize self-care and make choices that align with who we are and what we want. Above all, remember that our worth is not based on how much we do or achieve; it is about who we are as beloved daughters of the King.

In a world that never seems to slow down, embracing rest and balance may seem a bit rebellious, but it is a choice that will bring us true peace, joy, and fulfillment. Take a step back, take a deep breath, and fully embrace the rest and balance that we so desperately need in this drama queen world.

Radiating Inner Beauty

Being a kingdom princess has taught me a thing or two about beauty. True beauty comes from within and is like a radiance that cannot be dimmed by society's fickle trends.

To truly radiate inner beauty, you have to start with self-acceptance and self-love. We all have these unique qualities that make us who we are, and we have to learn to embrace them. No more comparing ourselves to others because we are fearfully and wonderfully made, my friend. We are these incredible masterpieces crafted by our heavenly Father, and it is up to us to honor and appreciate ourselves.

Along with accepting ourselves, inner beauty is about building up virtues and qualities that reflect the character of God (like patience, kindness, and compassion). When we cultivate these qualities, not only do they make our relationships with others amazing, but they also make our inner beauty shine on the outside.

Remember: we have to take time for ourselves. In the chaos of everyday life, it is so easy to forget how important those moments of solitude and reflection are, but those moments are like gold. Those are the moments when we can connect with our inner selves, figure out what we really want, and even commune with God. They are times for guidance, for becoming the best versions of ourselves.

Thankfulness is also a game-changer. When we take the time to be thankful for the little things, a shift happens. We stop focusing on what we lack and appreciate what we already have instead. It fills our hearts with contentment, which causes our inner beauty to really start to glow. Simple joys like a beautiful sunrise or a kind word remind us to appreciate the beauty around us. They bring fulfillment to our souls.

And here is the grand finale: live a purposeful life. When we align our actions and decisions with our values and beliefs, that is when we become the epitome of beauty. It is about pursuing our passions, using our gifts, and serving others. That is when our inner beauty becomes a beacon of hope and inspiration for those around us. They see us embracing our uniqueness and living with purpose, and it encourages them to do the same.

So, here I am, a kingdom princess in a world full of drama queens. My mission? To radiate inner beauty in a society that is obsessed with external appearances. I am able to do it by accepting myself, developing virtues, taking time for reflection, being grateful, and living a purposeful life. True beauty is not about flawless features; it is about having a heart filled with love, compassion, and a burning desire to make a positive difference in this world.

Time to Reflect

- Find a cozy spot, close your eyes, and just let all of the noise of the world fade away. Get lost in your own mind, in a place of peace and calm. Do you feel the warm embrace of God's love and acceptance? How does it make you feel?
- What does self-care really mean to you?
- Do you nurture your self-worth? If so, how?

Prayer

Dear God, please show me how to care about myself. Thank You that You are always with me, even if I do not acknowledge You. I pray that my life will be a reflection of Your love. Remind me to nurture my self-worth. Father, thank You that You have given me my life and for those around me. All this I ask in Jesus's name. Amen.

Chapter 7

Finding Purpose and Passion

I will instruct you and teach you in the way you should go; I will counsel you [who are willing to learn] with my Eye upon you.
Psalm 32:8 (AMP)

❦

Uncovering Your God-Given Purpose

UNCOVERING YOUR GOD-GIVEN purpose is a whole process of soul-searching, self-reflection, and being open to a higher calling. It is not for the faint of heart, but the rewards that come with finding your purpose are worth every bit of the struggle.

When I was diving into scripture, seeking some guidance and inspiration, I stumbled upon the story of Esther. She was something else – a woman with a backbone, a believer in the power of God, and she had enough courage in her veins to save her people. Talk about purpose hidden in some crazy palace politics!

Esther's story got me thinking, though. Our purpose is not always handed to us on a silver platter. Sometimes, it is all twisted up, hidden in the chaos of life, waiting for the right moment to be unraveled. Just like Esther found her purpose smack dab in the middle of a palace, we can find ours in this crazy world we live in – where drama queens reign and make their grand entrances.

Discovering our purpose means blocking out the noise around us and tuning into that small, quiet voice within. It is not about just having a job or playing a role in society; it is about finding our unique expression, our true selves, all woven into the very fabric of who we are.

In my journey to find my purpose, I had to do some soul-searching, digging into my passions, talents, and values. What makes my heart skip a beat? What brings me joy and fulfillment? What am I naturally good at? Asking these questions forced me to face my own desires and aspirations, free from the opinions and judgments of others.

Not only do we have to figure ourselves out, we also must align our lives with the teachings and principles of the scriptures to find our purpose. It is about seeking God's guidance through prayer, finding wisdom in mentors, and diving into theological studies. I knew that as a woman of God, my purpose was intricately tied to His plan for my life (Jer. 29:11).

Finding our purpose also means surrendering and trusting in something greater than ourselves. It means letting go of our own plans and agendas and submitting to God's will. It might push us outside our comfort zones, make us take some risks, and embrace the unknown. But when we have the guts to surrender our lives to God, He gives us the grace and strength to fulfill our purpose, even beyond our wildest dreams.

My friend, uncovering your God-given purpose is not a one-and-done type of thing; it is a lifelong journey of growth and discovery. It takes believing in your own worthiness, committing to constant self-improvement, and having a faith in God's incredible plan for your life.

Here is my challenge to you: take on this transformative journey. Dig deep into the scriptures, spend some quality time reflecting on yourself, and surrender yourself to God's will. Trust me, you will become a kingdom princess in this drama queen world, shining bright as a beacon of love, purpose, and grace.

Discovering Your Unique Gifts and Talents

Let me tell you about this whole concept of unique gifts and talents. It is not just some fancy mumbo jumbo. These things are what make us who we are. Gifts are the things we are naturally good at, like when you can paint your heart out or can pick up a guitar and just play it. Talents, on the other hand, are the skills we work on and get better at over time, like leadership or problem-solving.

Here is the thing: these gifts and talents are not just random happenings; they were deliberately put inside each of us by God. We were all made to do something amazing with the stuff we have, and the crazy part is, we have to go on this wild journey of self-discovery to unlock our full potential.

This journey is like a rollercoaster of emotions. You have to look deep within yourself and figure out who you really are. It is all about accepting that you are unique and super awesome in your own way because that is how God made you.

I started my journey by checking out what made me feel alive – my passions, hobbies, the stuff that made me feel like I was soaring - and that is when it hit me. I had this gift for communicating. I could talk, write, and get my thoughts across in a way that people could relate to. So, I decided to take it to the next level. I studied all kinds of stuff, from the Bible to psychology, to try and master this communication game: public speaking, engaging with all sorts of people, you name it. I found out I had this talent for empathy, too. I could connect with people on a deeper level and understand where they were coming from. It was like I had a sixth sense.

But this self-discovery thing is not all rainbows and kittens. Sometimes, you have to confront those limitations you have put on yourself. Society's expectations, your own doubts, and all of that noise can mess with your mind, but those limitations are not the boss of you. Your gifts and talents are not confined by that junk. They are a reminder that you are capable of epic stuff.

Embracing your gifts and talents is not just about discovering them; it is about accepting them, too. You must drop the comparisons, the insecurities, and the need for approval from others. Believe in yourself and be grateful for what you have. Your gifts are like gold, and they can make a real difference in this messed-up world.

As I stumbled through this drama queen world, I learned to unleash my gifts and talents. They became my strength and purpose. Communicating and empathizing with others not only made me stand out, it changed lives, too. Writing and speaking became my voice, and I stepped out of my comfort zone in an attempt to rock this role as a kingdom princess in this drama queen world.

So, as you start your own journey of self-discovery, go deep. Find those gifts and talents that are unique to you. Embrace and celebrate them because they are what make you so amazing. Remember: you were born to shine, no matter what this crazy world throws at you. It is through your gifts and talents that you will transform yourself and leave a mark on this wild ride we call life.

Pursuing Your Passions

When I was a young girl, I could not get enough of the arts. Creative outlets such as singing, dancing, and writing stories let me express myself in ways that words alone could not touch. And although I did not have the support to pursue these talents, I pursued them as best I could on my own. My first desk for writing was a little table in the basement where I could be alone with my thoughts.

As I got older, my love for the arts only grew stronger. Alongside that love, there was this nagging desire to understand God's Word on a deeper level. I had this burning curiosity to dive into sacred texts and discover the wisdom within, so that I could share it with others. That is what pushed me to pursue a bachelor's degree in biblical and theological studies and a minor in psychology to keep things interesting.

College turned out to be the perfect place for me to bring together my passion for the arts and my hunger for spiritual growth. I joined the worship team at my church and sharing my voice and leading others in worship was like a soul-deep connection. On top of that, I started a women's ministry at the church where we put on retreats. It was all about creating spaces where people could really feel the presence of God through their creative expression.

The biggest game-changer for me came the first time I stood in front of the congregation and bore my soul by telling my testimony. These people knew me, or they knew who I was at the time. I worried how they would accept me if they truly knew who I was or had been. I prayed to God to allow just one person to be touched by what I was going to share. I was welcomed with arms wide open. To say I was shocked would be an understatement, but it also awoke a passion that God had placed in me to write, to help those who are hurting and need to know that God loves them.

After I graduated, I knew deep down that I had a purpose. I had to keep sharing my life with others. No matter how uncomfortable it might be to speak or to write my story for others to hear or read, I saw God heal other women through my testimony. It was no longer about me; it was about the kingdom of God and showing other women that they, too, could be kingdom princesses.

Chasing your passions will not always be smooth sailing. There were times when doubt crept in, and I questioned whether I was on the right track. But I clung to Jeremiah 29:11 (NIV), "'For I know the plans I have for you,' declares the Lord, 'plans to prosper you and not to harm you, plans to give you hope and a future.'" In those moments, I reminded myself that my passions were not just about me; they were about serving God and serving others.

So, my dear princess, here is my advice to you: go after your passions with everything you have. Take the time to discover what sets your soul ablaze and do not be afraid to weave it into the fabric of your life. Seek guidance from God, trust in His wisdom, and know that you were made to impact this world in your own unique way. Pursue your passions, my princess warrior, and watch as you light up the world and find a sense of fulfillment that can only come from a deep, unshakeable faith.

Impacting the World with Your Purpose

As a woman of God, I have always felt this strong need to make a difference in the world, to leave my mark and bring some goodness into people's lives. In a world that is all about drama, it is so easy to get sucked into the chaos and lose sight of what really matters, but I have always believed that we have a higher calling as princesses of the kingdom. We were not made to just sit back and watch this whole show unfold. No, we were made to be the change-makers, the ones who bring light, love, and compassion into the lives of others.

Now, if we *really* want to make an impact, we first have to figure out what our purpose is. Our purpose is not being handed to us on a silver platter. It is more like a personalized blueprint that God has designed just for us. It is a beautiful combination of our passions, talents, and life experiences that is meant to bring about transformation in the world.

Discovering our purpose takes a lot of soul-searching and prayer, digging deep within ourselves, and seeking guidance from our heavenly Father. We have to let go of our own desires and ambitions and open ourselves up to becoming vessels through which God can work to impact the world.

Having a purpose is only the first step. It is all well and good to have these good intentions, but if we do not actually do something about it, then what is the point? That is why we have to take intentional action. We have to actively engage with the world around us and seek out opportunities to make a difference. Maybe it is volunteering at a local charity, starting a community outreach program, or using our talents to bring joy and inspiration to others. Whatever it is, we have to get out there and make it happen.

Impacting the world with our purpose is not just about what we do, though; it is about how we live our lives and the values we hold dear. We have to be a light in the darkness, showing love and kindness to everyone we meet. It is through our everyday interactions and relationships that we have the power to make a lasting impact on others.

As princesses of the kingdom, we cannot just follow the crowd. We have to be the influencers, the ones who change the narrative and shift the focus away from all of the drama. We have to show the world that there is a better way, that we can rise above all of the chaos, and bring about a positive change.

So, my fellow princesses, let us embrace our calling. Let us step up and make a real impact in the world with our purpose because, when we do, we not only fulfill our own destiny, but we also pave the way for others to do the same. Together, we can create a ripple effect of goodness and light that will transform this drama queen world into a kingdom where love reigns supreme.

Living a Life of Purpose and Passion

Sometimes, I sit and wonder, what does it really mean to live a life of purpose and passion? Like, deep-down-in-your-bones kind of living? I think it means living in sync with who we truly are - aligning our actions, goals, and values with what sets our souls on fire. It is waking up each morning all pumped up and ready to tackle the day because we know we are on a unique path that is meant just for us. It is finding that true sense of joy and fulfillment in the work we do, the relationships we build, and the impact we make in the world.

Finding our purpose takes some serious soul-searching, self-reflection, and the courage to dig deep into the very core of our being. We have to be open to discovering our passions, unearthing our desires, and facing our fears head-on. It is like slowly peeling back all of the layers of what other people expect from us, smashing through the chains of conformity, and embracing our true, authentic selves.

I remember when I first began my own journey to living a life full of purpose and passion. I thought I had it all figured out. I was going to college and thought my major and minor would give me that sense of purpose for which I was searching. But the more I dove into my studies, the more I started questioning if it really aligned with my deepest passions and desires.

Then, one day, I stumbled upon this quote by Howard Thurman that hit me like a freight train: "Don't ask yourself what the world needs. Ask yourself what makes you come alive, and go do that, because what the world needs is people who have come alive."[2] It was like a massive wake-up call, a reminder that true purpose and passion comes from within ourselves, not from what society expects from us.

With newfound determination burning in my veins, I set out on a quest to discover my true self. I dove into different hobbies and interests, experimenting with experiences that set my soul on fire. I went to workshops, devoured books, and had long chats with people who got what I was going through. I was not afraid to push myself beyond what was comfortable, nor did I let myself dream too big and believed that I could achieve great things.

Through all of that digging and exploring, I uncovered my true passions and desires. I found a love for writing and storytelling, a deep passion for empowering others through teaching and mentoring, and a burning desire to make a positive impact in the lives of those around me. Those discoveries not only brought me joy and fulfillment, but they gave me a sense of purpose that was bigger than just me.

Living a life of purpose and passion is not about reaching some certain level of success or accumulating piles of cash. It is about using our unique abilities and talents to make a positive difference in the world. It is about finding meaning in each and every moment and not getting too wrapped up in some far-off destination. It means embracing the challenges and setbacks that come our way, knowing that they are just opportunities for growth and self-discovery.

Now, this whole purpose and passion thing is not a final destination you reach and then hang up your hat. It is a lifelong commitment, a journey that keeps evolving and changing as we grow. It requires us to constantly reflect, reevaluate, and adjust. It takes resilience, persistence, and a willingness to face the unknown head-on. Most importantly, it requires us to trust ourselves and have faith in the divine plan unfolding in front of us.

So, go on and start your own journey to living a life of purpose and passion. Take the time to really explore and embrace your desires, passions, and deepest dreams. Embrace what makes you shine and let yourself come alive in a world that is so often suffocating. Trust the process because you have the power inside you to create a life that is meaningful, joyful, and full of purpose. Remember: you are a princess in a world full of drama queens, and your purpose and passion are just waiting to be set free.

Time to Reflect

- Have you found your purpose in life? If not, what can you do to discover it?
- Do you know what your gifts and talents are? If so, what are they?
- What is your deepest passion? How can you act on it as a kingdom princess?

Prayer

Father, thank You for all that You do for me. Help me to discover what my purpose in life is. Please forgive me if I have fallen short in this aspect and help me to discover what it is that You would have me do. Help me to discover my passion. I ask all of this in Jesus's name. Amen.

Conclusion

Embracing Your Kingdom Calling

For all the law is fulfilled in one word, even in this: "You shall love your neighbor as yourself."

Galatians 5:14 (NKJV)

Discovering Your Kingdom Calling

THE WHOLE IDEA of a kingdom calling can seem pretty out there and hard to grasp, but it is a life-changer. It is not a job or title you aim for, but more like a divine invite, a call to fulfill your God-given purpose in this crazy world we live in.

To really wrap your head around this kingdom calling stuff, you have to understand the bigger picture. The kingdom of God is not some physical place with borders; it is a spiritual realm where God is holding it down. It is a place of goodness, peace, and joy through the Holy Spirit, and as God's daughters, we are part of this heavenly kingdom.

Our kingdom calling is deeply rooted in who God is. He made each of us unique with special gifts, talents, and passions, all meant to be used for His glory. Like the way a kingdom needs experts in different fields, God has given us specific roles and responsibilities that fit into His grand plan (1 Cor. 12:4-6).

Discovering our kingdom calling is going to take some soul-searching, prayer, and leaning on God for guidance. It starts with knowing who we are as God's daughters and realizing our worth is not based on what others think. Our calling is not about getting famous, rich, or successful; it is about embracing our true purpose as ambassadors of God's kingdom.

Finding our kingdom calling also means giving up our selfish desires and trading them in for God's will. It is about letting go of our own plans and trusting that God knows best. It might push us out of our comfort zones, nudge us to take risks, and require some serious faith, but by doing this, we are aligning ourselves with the incredible story God is writing in our lives.

And do not forget, the power of community is a force to be reckoned with on this journey. Surrounding ourselves with fellow believers who build us up and cheer us on is an important part. Together, we can share our struggles, dreams, and victories, and challenge one another to live out our calling to the max.

But listen up, sister. Discovering our kingdom calling is not the end of the road. It is going to be a lifelong adventure of growing, learning, and obeying. Our calling might shift and change as we move through different seasons of life, but as long as we stay rooted in God's truth and remain open to His leading, we can be sure our purpose will bear fruit.

So, my dear princesses, I am begging you, do not pass up on this journey of discovering your kingdom calling. Dive deep into your heart, let go of your plans, and lean on God every step of the way because by embracing your true purpose, not only will you find fulfillment, but you will also become a living example of God's love and power in this world full of drama queens.

Using Your Influence for Good

Let me tell you something I have discovered on this crazy journey of mine. Influence is not just about having power or being in charge. It is about how we choose to live our lives, the decisions we make, and the values we hold dear. As a princess in this kingdom, I have learned that my influence reaches further than I ever imagined, like a ripple effect touching the lives of others in ways I never thought possible.

But using our influence for good takes some serious self-reflection. We need to check our hearts and motivations. Are we just looking for power, or are we genuinely driven to make a positive impact in the world? This self-examination is so important because it is only when our hearts are aligned with God's that we can truly change lives.

It takes courage to use our influence in the right way. In a world filled with drama queens, it can be tough to stand up for what is right, challenge the norm, and speak truth in the face of opposition. But us princesses are meant to be bold and unyielding in our pursuit of justice, mercy, and righteousness. We cannot let fear or other people's opinions hold us back from making a difference.

Here is the issue: using our influence is not just about grand gestures or doing huge acts of service; it is about the little choices we make every single day that can have a huge impact on those around us. It is about choosing kindness over cruelty, forgiveness over bitterness, and love over hate. Our words have power, too. They can lift others up, inspire their dreams, and speak life into their situations.

But do you know what is really powerful? Prayer. As princesses, we have a direct line to the King of Kings, and prayer is our secret weapon against all of the darkness in the world. When we pray for our families, friends, communities, and the whole world, we are tapping into something supernatural (Phil. 4:6-7). We are inviting God to step in and make some serious changes.

Being a princess in a world full of drama requires purpose, courage, and a whole lot of intentionality, but when we fully embrace our calling as influencers for good, we become amazing change-makers in a world that desperately needs it. So, let us align our hearts with God's, step out in faith, and use our influence wisely. Together, we can create a world that is more beautiful, just, and filled with love.

Serving Others with Humility

Humility is not just about being meek and mild; it is about a whole mindset of putting others before ourselves. It is about realizing that we are not the center of the universe, but rather just a small piece of the big picture. And to be truly humble, we have to let go of our egos, our need for attention, and all of those selfish desires. Instead, we choose to serve others willingly and joyfully without expecting anything in return.

As a woman of God, with all of my biblical and theological studies under my belt, I have come to understand that serving others with humility is deeply rooted in the teachings of Jesus Christ. He was the epitome of humility. He washed the feet of His disciples, showing us that true greatness in His kingdom is all about being a servant (John 13:5). And He was always telling His followers to love and serve one another, just like He did.

But in this drama queen world where everyone is all about promoting themselves and putting themselves first, humility can be seen as a weakness. It is anything but weak. It is the strength that sets us apart as princesses in God's kingdom. Yes, the world might push us to compete and seek power and recognition, but as daughters of the King, we are called to a different standard. We have to live with humble hearts and look for ways to serve and bless others.

Now, practicing humility is going to take a whole lot of love for people for it is about seeing the worth and value in every single person. When we serve with humility, we do not look down on anyone, we meet them where they are. We embrace their struggles and offer a hand. We want to lift them up and give them a boost, not tear them down or treat them like they are beneath us.

And serving others with humility does not mean neglecting ourselves. It is a tricky balance for we need to take care of ourselves. We need to set boundaries and make sure we are not sacrificing our own well-being. We need to watch our motivations, too. Our acts of service have to come from a genuine desire to love and care for others, not just from a need to impress or gain approval.

But when we serve others with humility, it is like a superpower. It transforms us and the ones we serve. It opens doors to real connections and deepens our compassion. It helps us appreciate the beauty in God's diverse creation and brings us all together in unity and harmony.

So, my fellow princesses, let us rise up and embrace this call to serve with humility. Let us step out of our comfort zones, put our pride aside, and invest our time, energy, and resources into acts of service because that is how we truly reflect the heart of our Father and experience the abundant life He has called us to live.

Leaving a Lasting Legacy

As I ponder the true meaning of leaving behind a legacy, I realize that it is essential to understand the context in which this concept exists. In a world that is constantly chasing fleeting trends and yearning for instant gratification, it is easy to lose sight of the bigger picture. We get so caught up in our personal ambitions and desires that we often forget about the impact we have on others and the world around us.

Leaving a lasting legacy goes far beyond our own lifetime. It surpasses the boundaries of time, reaching out to the generations to come. It is about recognizing that our actions today possess the power to shape the world tomorrow. It is about living with purpose and intention and passing on our values to the ones who follow.

As someone who feels like a princess in a world full of drama queens, I find guidance in the principles instilled in me through my faith and education. Throughout my journey, I have come to understand that leaving a lasting legacy requires embracing love, compassion, and selflessness. It is about nurturing the connections we make and finding ways to positively impact the lives of those around us.

Leaving a legacy is not just about the grand gestures that influential figures are often remembered for. It can manifest itself in the simplest of actions, in the way we connect with others and inspire them. It is about contributing to the greater good, regardless of how big or small our platform may be.

Ensuring that our legacy endures, that it creates a ripple effect beyond our own existence, boils down to one word: authenticity. When we live as our true selves and stay true to our values, our legacy becomes a true reflection of who we are at our core. It becomes a manifestation of our beliefs, passions, and purpose.

Leaving a lasting legacy is not a destination to be reached; it is a lifelong journey. It requires us to constantly reflect on ourselves, grow, and commit ourselves to making a difference in the world. It is about embracing the power within us to leave a positive and profound mark on the lives of others.

As I reflect on the significance of leaving a lasting legacy, I am reminded of the wise words of Maya Angelou, who once said, "I've learned that people will forget what you said, people will forget what you did, but people will never forget how you made them feel."[3] In these words, we find the true essence of leaving a lasting legacy: it is the impact we have on the hearts and souls of others.

So, let us strive to be more than just fleeting shadows in this drama-filled world. Let us be kingdom princesses who leave behind a legacy of love, compassion, and inspiration. Let us embrace the responsibility we have to shape a better world for future generations. And let us never underestimate the power we hold within us to make a lasting and transformative difference.

Embracing God's Calling

It all started at that moment. That moment when it hit me like a truck, telling me to give my whole life to God. I remember it so clearly, like it was just yesterday. There was this pull on my heart that I could not ignore, this voice in my head screaming that I needed to follow my faith and serve in ministry. Trust me when I say it was not an easy decision to make for this path I was choosing demanded everything from unwavering devotion to sacrifice after sacrifice. But there was this fire burning so fiercely within me, and I knew deep down that this was the moment I had been waiting for my entire life.

With my bachelor's degree, I felt ready to dive headfirst into this God-given calling. I wanted to immerse myself in His Word and tackle the doubts and uncertainties that tried to creep in. It became a season of deep soul-searching. A time where I really discovered my gifts and talents, the things that would form the foundation of everything I was meant to do.

This journey of embracing my calling, however, was not an easy task to accomplish. There were moments when I felt like the weight of the world was crushing me; the expectations and responsibilities were all so overwhelming. I started doubting myself, questioning if I had what it took to live out this grand purpose, but in those moments of weakness, I learned to lean on God and trust in His strength and guidance. He became my rock, the one I turned to when I felt like I was drowning.

Embracing this calling was no one-time decision, but rather a constant surrender, a daily commitment to seek His wisdom and align my desires with His. I have to step out in faith, even when I cannot see a clear path ahead. The more I let go and give control to God, the more I watch His plan unfold in front of me.

And embracing my calling was not just about me and God. It meant opening my eyes to the needs of the people around me, becoming a servant. It meant having a heart full of compassion, empathy, and love that overflowed. I had to be ready to help those who were hurting, to be the hands and feet of God in a broken world. And let me tell you, there is nothing more rewarding or fulfilling than being a vessel of His grace. It is like I am bringing a taste of heaven on earth.

Society throws so many expectations our way, trying to make us blend in or conform. But for me, embracing my calling means standing firm in who I am and what I believe, even when people make fun of me or try to tear me down. It means saying no to the superficial stuff and saying yes to the real stuff like honor, integrity, and humility over fame and fortune.

As I sit here and reflect on my journey, I cannot help but feel so grateful. I mean, seriously, me? I am flawed and messy, but God chose me to be His representative, His love and grace in this messed-up world. Each step I take toward fulfilling my purpose is proof of His faithfulness and the incredible power of living a life submitted to His will.

So, my friend, I am telling you right now to go on your own journey of embracing your calling. It will not always be easy, and you will question yourself sometimes, but you are not alone. God has given you a unique purpose, and He is going to give you everything you need to make it happen. Embrace that calling, my friend. Be bold with it because in doing so, you will find a life full of fulfillment, joy, and something that lasts beyond the here and now.

Time to Reflect

- You are God's daughter. What does that mean to you?
- Are you using your influence for good? If so, how?
- Are you leaving a lasting legacy? What is your legacy?

Prayer

Dear Lord, You are awesome and glorious. Thank You for all that You have done in my life. Please help me to remember that I am a daughter of the King. Give me patience and the ability to show Your love to others. Help me to leave a lasting legacy that brings glory to Your name. I pray this in Jesus's name. Amen.

Scriptures

ை

- *Then God said, "Let us make man in Our image, according to Our likeness; Let them have dominion over the fish of the sea, over the birds of the air, and over the cattle, over all the earth and over every creeping thing that creeps on the earth.* Genesis 1:26 (NKJV)
- *So God created man in His own image; in the image of God he created them; male and female He created them.* Genesis 1:27 (NKJV)
- *But the Lord said to Samuel, "Do not look at his appearance or at the height of his stature, because I have rejected him; for God does not see as man sees, since man looks at the outward appearance, but the Lord looks at the heart.* 1 Samuel 16:7 (NASB)
- *I will instruct you and teach you, in the way you should go; I will counsel you [who are willing to learn] with My eye upon you.* Psalm 32:8 (AMP)
- *From the ends of the earth, I cry to you for help when my heart is overwhelmed. Lead me to the towering rock of safety, for you are my safe refuge, a fortress where my enemies cannot reach me.* Psalm 61:2-3 (NLT)
- *You who still the noise of the seas, the noise of their waves, and the tumult of the peoples.* Psalm 65:7 (NKJV)

- *I praise you, for I am fearfully and wonderfully made; marvelous are your works and that my soul knows very well.* Psalm 139:14 (NKJV)
- *Above all else, guard your heart, for everything you do flows from it.* Proverbs 4:23 (NIV)
- *Make no friendship with an angry man, and with a furious man do not go, lest you learn his ways and set a snare for your soul.* Proverbs 22:24-25 (NKJV)
- *Fear not, for I am with you; be no dismayed, for I am your God. I will strengthen you, yes, I will help you, I will uphold you with my righteous right hand.* Isaiah 41:10 (NKJV)
- *For I know the thoughts that I think toward you, says the Lord, thoughts of peace and not of evil, to give you a future and a hope.* Jeremiah 29:11 (NKJV)
- *And whenever you stand praying, if you have anything against anyone, forgive him, that your Father in heaven may also forgive your trespasses. But if you do not forgive, neither will your Father in heaven forgive your trespasses.* Mark 11:25-26 (NKJV)
- *After that, He poured water into a basin and began to wash the disciples' feet, and to wipe them with the towel with which He was girded.* John 13:5 (NKJV)
- *So now there is no condemnation for those who belong to Christ Jesus.* Romans 8:1 (NLT)
- *And we know that all things work together for good to them that love God, to them who are the called according to his purpose.* Romans 8:28 (NLT)
- *And do not be conformed to this world, but be transformed by the renewing of your mind, that you may prove what is that good and acceptable and perfect will of God.* Romans 12:2 (NKJV)
- *Do you not know that your bodies are temples of the Holy Spirit, who is in you, whom you have received from God? You are not your own; you were bought at a price. Therefore honor God with your bodies.* 1 Corinthians 6:19-20 (NIV)

- *There are diversities of gifts, but the same Spirit. There are differences of ministries, but the same Lord. And there are diversities of activities, but it is the same God who works all in all.* 1 Corinthians 12:4-6 (NKJV)
- *Therefore, if anyone is in Christ, he is a new creation; old things have passed away; behold, all things have become new. Now all things are of God, who has reconciled us to Himself through Jesus Christ, and has given us the ministry of reconciliation, that is, that God was in Christ reconciling the world to Himself, not imputing their trespasses to them, and has committed to us the word of reconciliation. Now then, we are ambassadors for Christ, as though God were pleading through us: we implore you on Christ's behalf, be reconciled to God.* 2 Corinthians 5:17-20 (NKJV)
- *For all the law is fulfilled in one word, even in this: "You shall love your neighbor as yourself."* Galatians 5:14 (NKJV)
- *And be kind to one another, tenderhearted, forgiving one another, even as God in Christ forgave you.* Ephesians 4:32 (NKJV)
- *I can do all things through Christ who strengthens me.* Philippians 4:13 (NKJV)
- *Be anxious for nothing, but in everything by prayer and supplication, with thanksgiving, let your request be made known to God; and the peace of God, which surpasses all understanding, will guard your hearts and minds through Christ Jesus.* Philippians 4:6-7 (NKJV)
- *But you are chosen people, a royal priesthood, a holy nation, God's special possession, that you may declare the praises of him who called you out of darkness into his wonderful light.* 1 Peter 2:9 (NIV)
- *See what kind of love the Father has given us, that we should be called children of God; and so we are. The reason why the world does not know us is that it did not know him.* 1 John 3:1 (ESV)

References

❦

1. Vicki Bower, "Mind-body research moves towards the mainstream," February 25, 2024, https://www.ncbi.nlm.nih.gov/pmc/articles/PMC1456909/

2. "40 Quotes by Howard Thurman That Shaped a Movement," Daily Brightside, September 29, 2021, https://dailybrightside.com/40-quotes-by-howard-thurman-that-shaped-a-movement/.

3. Maya Angelou, "I Know Why the Caged Bird Sings Quotes by Maya Angelou," Goodreads, accessed November 10, 2023, https://www.goodreads.com/work/quotes/1413589-i-know-why-the-caged-bird-sings.

Milton Keynes UK
Ingram Content Group UK Ltd.
UKHW022334050624
443649UK00017BA/1061

9 781662 897191